Welcome to Destiny Roberts Books

Enjoy the journey with Destiny's Books.

Thank you for choosing this Destiny activity book!

Our goal is to inspire, encourage, and uplift children as they learn, grow, and explore the world around them.

Each page is thoughtfully designed to promote:

Creativity

Confidence

Curiosity

Whether it's coloring, solving puzzles, or trying something new, every activity is a small step forward in your child's journey.

We hope this book brings joy, sparks imagination, and encourages pride in every little accomplishment along the way.

The Fun Doesn't Stop Here!

We're busy creating even more exciting workbooks to keep young minds active and inspired all year long!

Coming Summer 2025:

Dino Discovery Days

Jungle Adventures

Vroom! Cars & Trucks Workbook

Under the Sea Explorers

Desert Animal Activity Book

Because big imaginations deserve big adventures.

FOR THE MOMS WHO HUG US TIGHTER,
CHEER US LOUDER, AND LOVE US BIGGER
THAN THE WORLD ITSELF. THIS BOOK IS
FOR YOU.

This Book belongs to :

_____

Table of Contents

- Goodbye for now
- We thank you

Coloring Pages

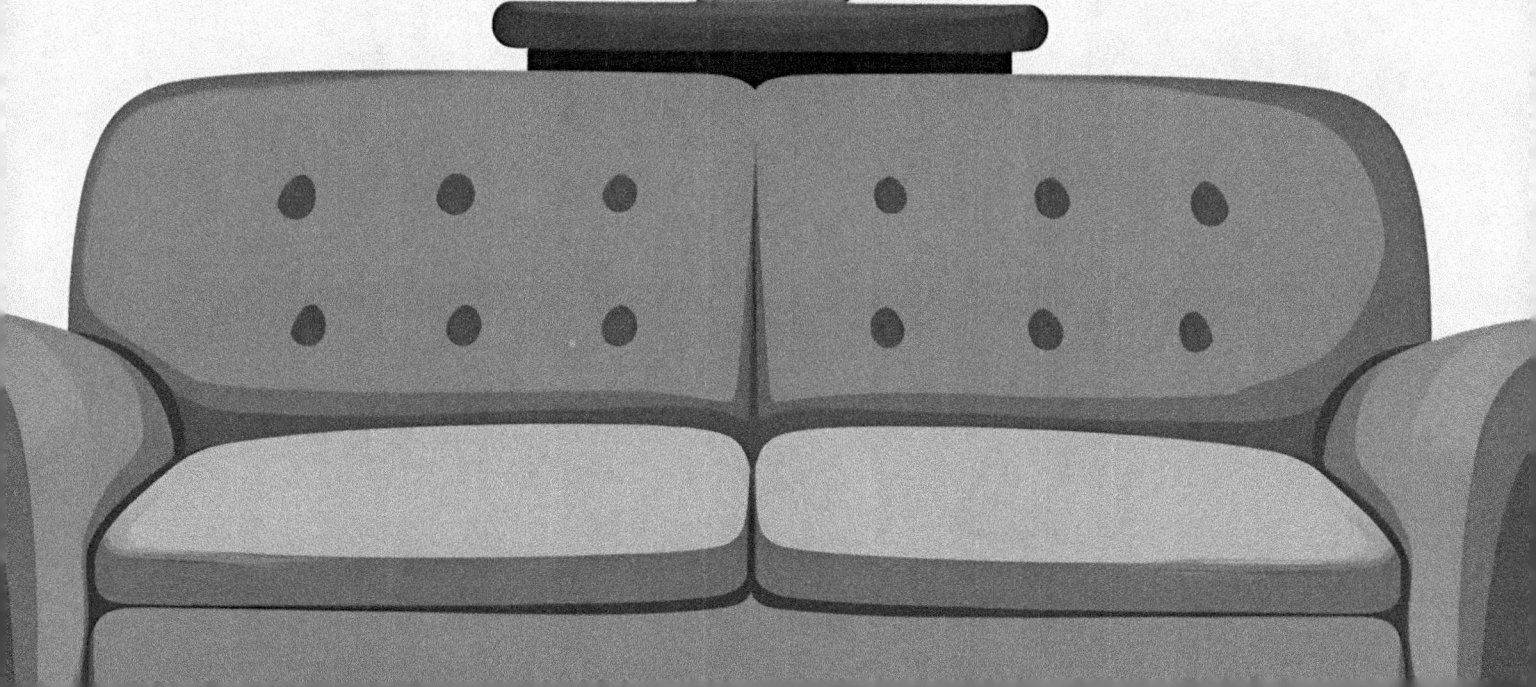

Mom loves fresh flowers.

Mom trusts her heart.....

Hummingbirds make Mom smile.

11

Our mom is the best mom ever!

Best Mom
Ever!!!

Mom relaxes at the spa.

Mom at her favorite beauty spa.

Happy Mom

14

For you, Mom.

15

Dad gives mom a bottle of her favorite perfume.

We take mom out for dinner on her special day.

mmmmmmm...we love making cookies!

18

Mom shopping at her favorite store.

19

Think & Tell
Sect 2

I want to draw a picture of my amazing mom:

Parenting is my mom's super power. Let me tell you how she does it.

Awards and Coupons

Congratulating our winners!

Join uls in congratulating our winners!

Gold Award Winner: (Name)

Silver Award Winner: (Name)

Broze Award Winner: (Name)

Special Thank   for all your exclusive participants!

My mom gets the "Best Mom Ever" award from our family!

Best Mom Ever

Roses for Mom.

26

Coupons for you, Mom.

More free loving than even before

A 30 min back rub with alochol and oil after work on when you feel like it.

A Day off from cooking. We got you, Mom!

A free trip to the message polar of your choice for an hour.

Mazes

Help Mom escape the nightmare
of chores...

Puzzle 1

Mom needs a path from home to the spa....

Puzzle 2

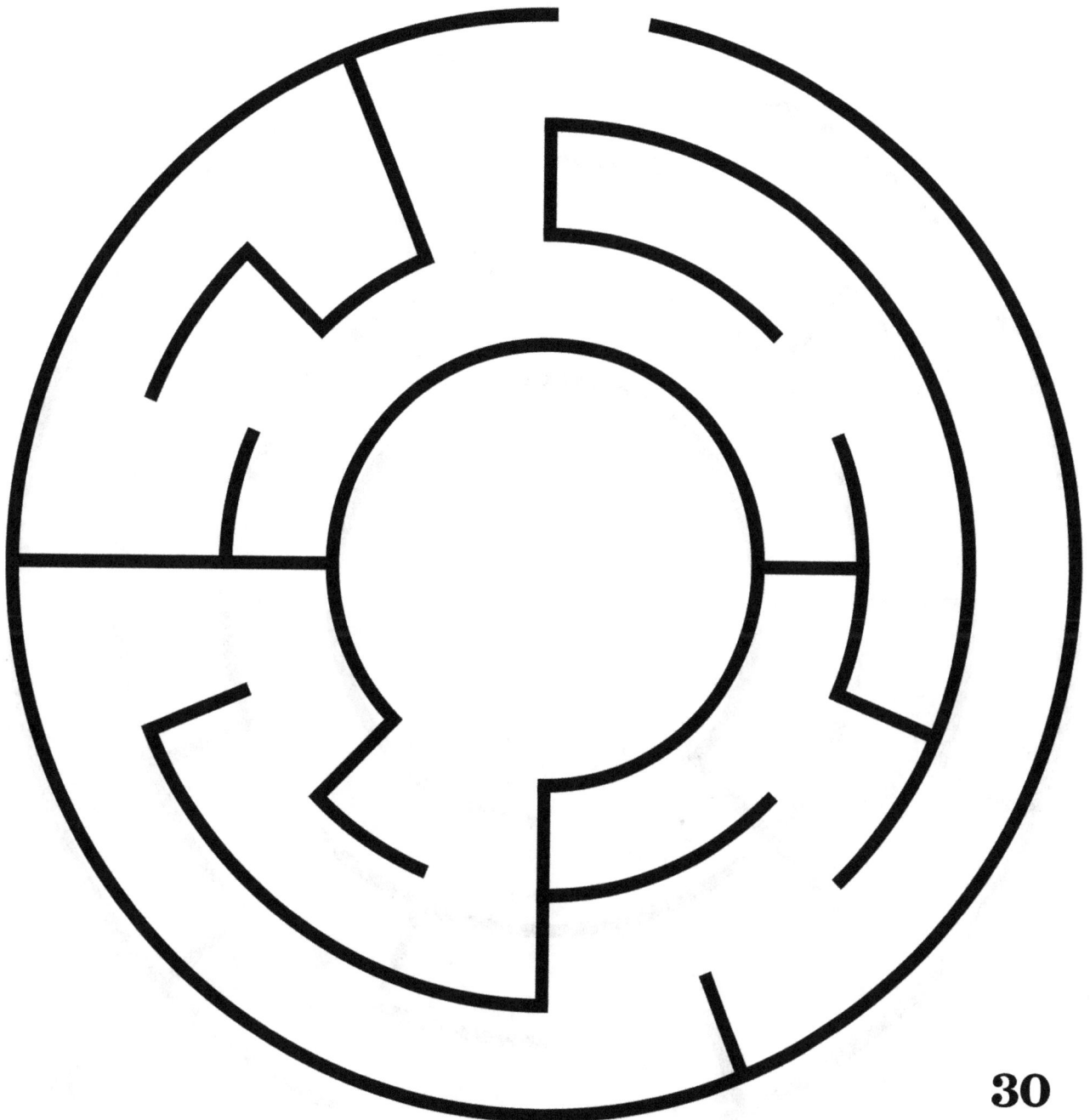

Mom needs needs a bread from cooking dinner tonight....let's take her out tonight.

Puzzle 3

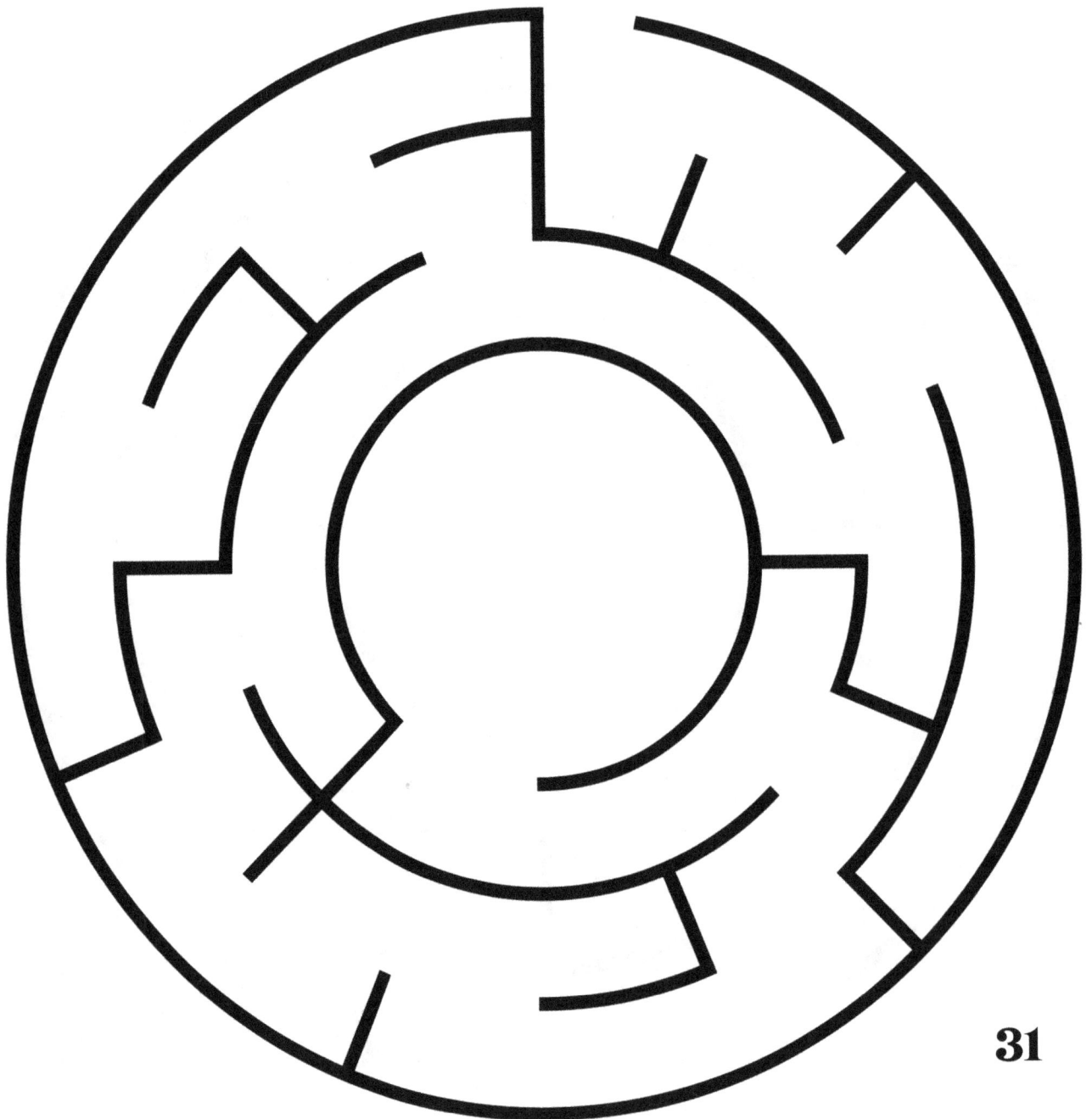

Mom needs a break from paying the bills...let's treat her to a night at the theatre.

Puzzle 4

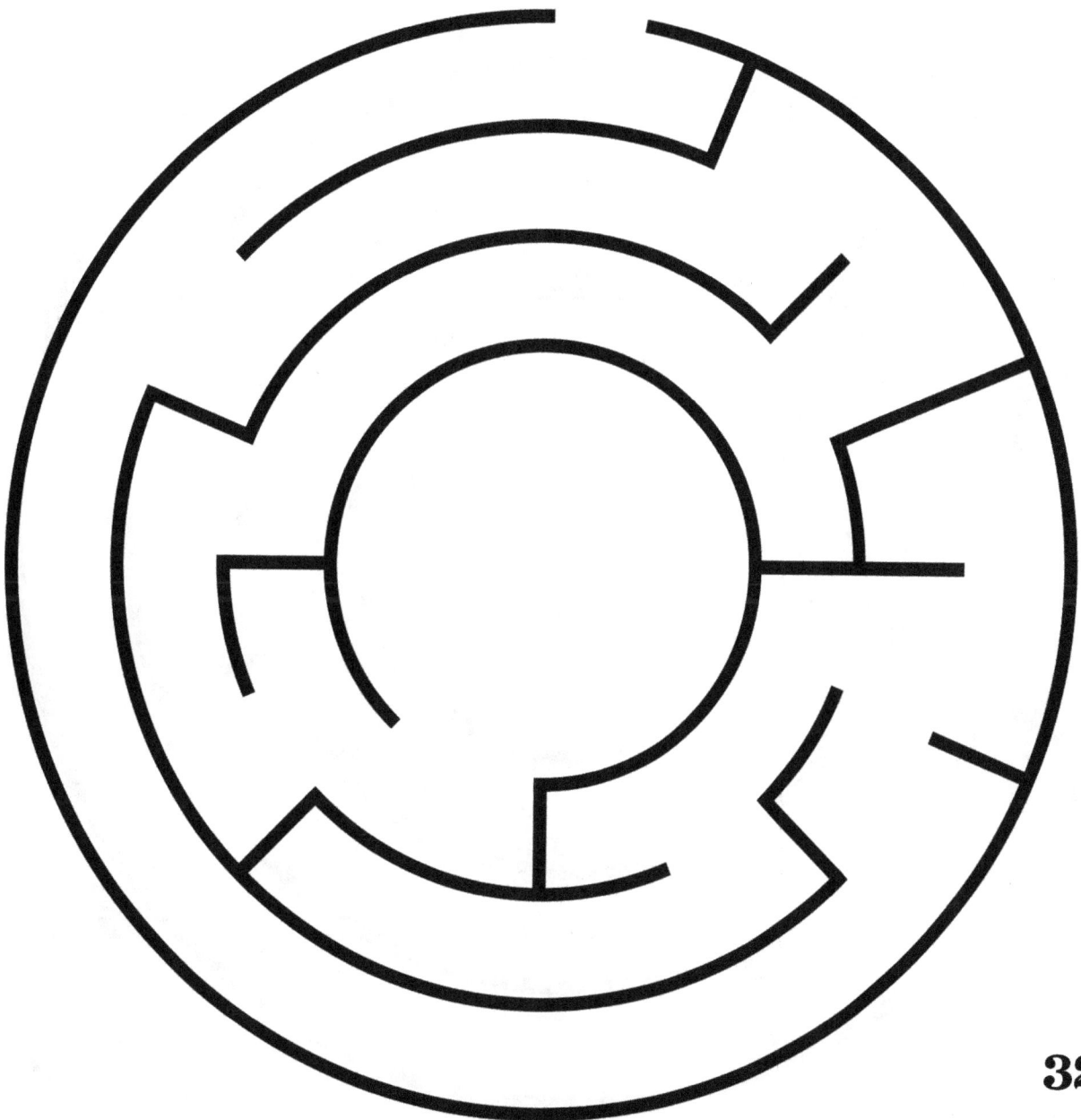

It's mom's turn to provide snacks for our soccer team. Let's load them in the car for her.

Puzzle 5

Maze
Solutions

Help Mom escape the nightmare
of chores...

Puzzle 1

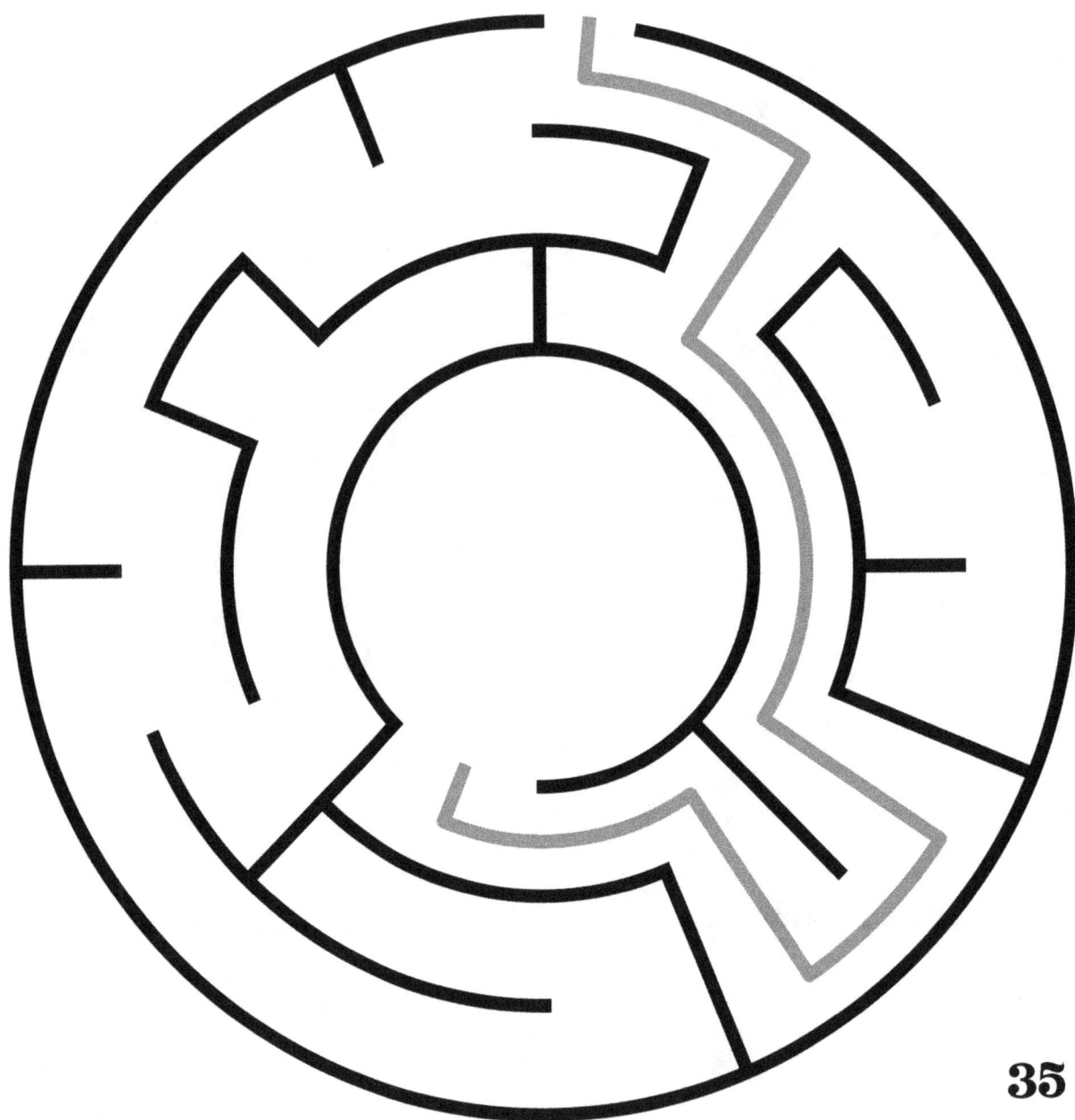

Mom needs a path from home to
the spa....

Puzzle 2

Mom needs needs a bread from cooking dinner tonight....let's take her out tonight.

Puzzle 3

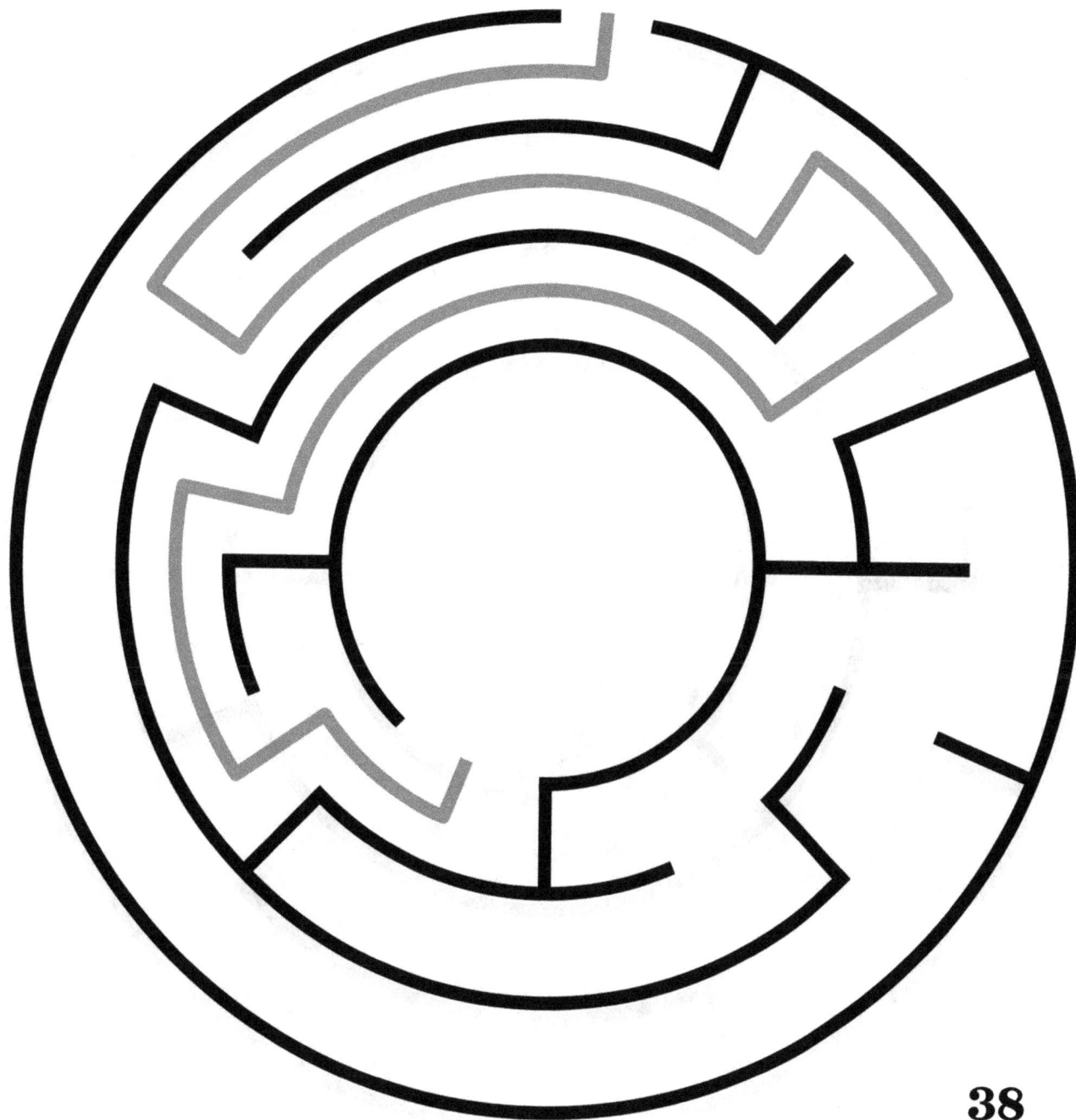

Mom needs a break from paying the bills...let's treat her to a night at the theatre.

Puzzle 4

It's mom's turn to provide snacks for our
soccer team. Let's load them in the car
for her.

Puzzle 5

Goodbye for Now! 💜

Thank you for spending time with us and creating special memories just for Mom.
 We hope you had fun coloring, writing, thinking, and celebrating the amazing woman in your life!
Don't worry — we'll be back with more exciting books and activities soon.
 Until then... keep smiling, keep learning, and keep spreading love wherever you go!

Thank You for Joining Us! 🪶

We're so glad you came along on this special Mother's Day journey.

Whether you colored a masterpiece, wrote a sweet note, or made Mom smile with a coupon, you created something truly meaningful.

At Sydni Readers, we believe in celebrating love, family, and learning — one fun page at a time.

We hope you'll join us again soon for more adventures, more imagination, and more ways to show the people you love just how special they are. 💕

www.ingramcontent.com/pod-product-compliance
Lightning Source LLC
Chambersburg PA
CBHW081553040426

42448CB00016B/3309